I Left The Faucet

Running

And Other
Poems For Kids

**Poems by
James Langston Jr**

**Illustrated by
Adam Quintanilla**

AuthorHouse™
1663 Liberty Drive
Bloomington, IN 47403
www.authorhouse.com
Phone: 1 (800) 839-8640

Published by AuthorHouse 03/25/2019

ISBN: 978-1-7283-0561-5 (sc)
ISBN: 978-1-7283-0562-2 (e)

Print information available on the last page.

Image on page 25 was taken with permission from Gettyimages.com

This book is printed on acid-free paper.

authorHOUSE®

The Dedication

Justice (Alex) L., Cadence B.,
Addison L., Samuel C. W.
The teachers and students of Cogburn
Woods Elementary School Alpharetta GA
My Janus Team Erbil Iraq
-J.L.

In memory of my father Javier Quintanilla

-A.Q.

A Mess

Why does mom wear those polka dots?

The fabric with a thousand spots

She stays covered in it from head to toe

Why does she like it I don't know?

I think she's putting on a show

Whether on a pair of pants or dress

Those polka dots just look a mess.

New Friends!!

Another Friend

What I did on my summer vacation

is enough to fill a book

I searched for buried treasure its archived take a look

I packed on a pound of muscle each week I hit the gym

I learned to speak a new language

I even learned to swim

I ate a gallon of ice cream, had shakes and burgers too

And rode the tallest coaster, took

a trip to the local zoo

I took a class on baking but burned every single batch

And chartered a giant fishing boat to

see how many fish I could catch

What I did on my summer vacation I hated for it to end

I planted a flower garden and made another friend.

Chores

Sometimes I have to mow the lawn

And rake the leaves until they're gone

Walk the dog and wash the car

Clean the drive way near and far

Straighten the corners of the shed

Dust below and overhead

Scrub the toilet and the tub

Give the brass an extra rub

Wash the curtains, fold the clothes

Put everything back in the place it goes

Wash all the windows, mop the floors

These are just a few of my chores.

Class President

No more homework! No more test!

I promise that I'll do my best

To minimize our workload here

You'll get to wear your favorite gear

The lunchroom ladies won't be rude

They'll only serve us catered food

We'll get an hour for our lunch

So we can chat, hangout and munch

Our favorite music will be played

And no field trips will be delayed

If you want to take the day off be my guest

And if you get tired take a rest

Each day would be a show and tell

If I am picked all will go well

From now until the school years done

I guarantee we will have fun

I promise that I'll represent

If you elect me class president.

Get Home

The lunchroom lady serves up

things I wouldn't feed a dog

Some items rough or even tough as

a bump you'd see on a log

You cannot tell that icky smell like

something on the lawn

When you hear the bell it is not

well, your appetite is gone

Most kids sit still and some get ill,

while others stand or roam

But many wait to hit the gate and

eat when they get home.

I Left The Faucet Running

I left the faucet running and that was a huge mistake

The water just kept going now it's flowing like a lake

The house is saturated not a single inch is dry

My parents are both angry and I am the reason why

I knew I should've listen but I didn't stop to think

Of all the precious water that was

coming from the sink

I knew that I was grounded this was not a tiny spill

There's no way my allowance can erase the water bill.

I Think I'll Stay At Home Today

I think I'll stay at home today I will not go to school

I don't want to follow directions or obey a single rule

I will not carry a binder or wait outside for the bus

No need to open a locker or hear my teachers fuss

I think I'll stay in bed today and barely move around

I do not know what else to say but silence is a sound.

If I Were King

If I were a king I'd sit and I'd rule

The first thing I'd do is eliminate school

I'd get rid of homework and every last chore

Like cleaning and dishes we'd do that no more

There would be no curfew, no rules to discuss

I'd make it so grownups would listen to us

We'd eat what we want to and do what we like

A bucket of ice cream, no helmet, a bike

The list would be endless now wouldn't that be cool

If I were a king with a kingdom to rule.

<u>Last</u>

Winners win that's what they do

And losers have a routine too

They never push they love to slack

And always end up on their back

They come up with an excuse why

They never win they never try

They love to give up far too fast

That's why they always come in last.

My Best Friend Is A Lazy Bug

My best friend is a lazy bug

He's stationary as a rug

He is the king of all things slack

His favorite position is on his back

I guess you can say he is a slob

He falls asleep on every job

He won't lift a finger to pick up dirt

I don't know why he's so inert

Why does he have to be so dull?

What's going on inside his skull?

If rewards were given he'd earn the title

Of the one they'd label the most idle

He really likes to procrastinate, that's

the reason why he's always late

He's more lackluster than a moth

He's ten times slower than a sloth

He's a lazy bug but in the end

I'm proud to say he's my best friend.

My Brother Is An Alien

My brother is an alien he's not like you or me

He loves to eat his vegetables and

does his chores for free

He's into science fiction and he's always reading books

He's not taken by fashion but he cares about his looks

His bank account is big enough

to choke a horse or cow

When others need advice they come

to him to show them how

He's really good with numbers

does equations in his head

He fixed my dad's computer and

planted mom a flowerbed

He also does experiments and wears these funny hats

He keeps a raccoon as a pet and even studies bats

That's why I think he's strange and I

have got the strongest case

My brother is an alien he comes from outerspace.

My Dog Ate My Homework

My dog ate my homework you heard what I said

He chewed up the papers I had by the bed

It took me three hours until I was through

Now I'm left with nothing so what will I do?

I have no excuses for parents or teachers

Should I call a lawyer should I call a preacher?

My dog ate my homework because he's a goof

My dog ate my homework but I don't have proof.

My Fault

I think I may have flunked a test

I know I didn't do my best

I didn't take a single note

And now I'm in a shaky boat

This is bad decision made

I need to get a passing grade

There was no reason for me to shirk

Like others I should do the work

If the outcome is an adverse result

The blames on me, it is my fault.

My Grandma Is A Hoarder

My grandma is a hoarder that makes living very hard

You cannot see the front door for

the clutter in the yard

We've tried to get her help but she's

attached to useless goods

Her property is covered from the

backdoor to the woods

There's hardly any room inside the

house to move around

Her feet don't hit the floor because

she cannot see the ground

The neighbors all complain they

say it's just a big eye sore

She cannot entertain that's not an option anymore.

My Grandma Knows Karate

My grandma knows karate and she knows jujitsu too

She just received a title as a black belt in kung-fu

She's into sumo wrestling and she is a samurai

Her boxing skills are such that she

makes all opponents cry

My grandma is a warrior my granny isn't slow

She'll take you down with fancy moves

she learned in taekwondo

If you see her coming from the gym

you best move out her way

She's just got finished training on the mats for mma

She's a bullseye with an arrow and

she's deadly with a sword

She takes all of the classes that

her pension can afford.

<u>My Lower Back Is Killing Me</u>

My lower back is killing me I don't know what I did

It's not supposed to be like this because I'm just a kid

Because I like to run and flip or wrestle in the dirt

It's not my job to have a care or fear of being hurt

My lower back is killing me I don't what to do

If you perform a reckless stunt your

back would kill you too.

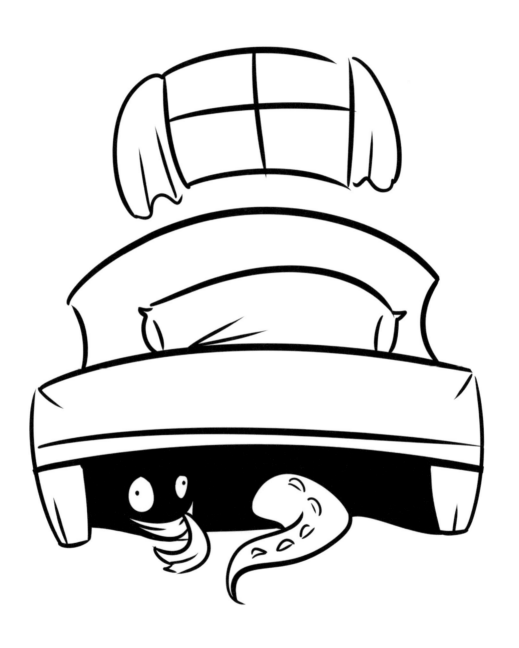

My Science Project Got Away

My science project got away it

broke free from the glass

I saw it go beneath the door and

slither across the grass

It took me weeks to create it I made it in a dish

To me it was the best one yet a mix of snake and fish

I wonder what I'm going to do.

Today my science project is due.

Practice

Practice makes perfect that's what they say

My sister does this everyday

The moment we get home from school

Standing or sitting on a stool

It's starting to drive me up a wall

The torture coming up the hall

It makes me grit I cannot grin

My sister on the violin.

Prepare

In school whenever we have a test

It's then that I get little rest

My mind combs over tons of facts

My eyes scans pages of books in stacks

I dot my I's and make my t's straight

And every night I stay up late

The grade I get needs to be square

And that's the reason I prepare.

The Summer Is Over

The summer is over and it was cool

Now it's time for us to go back to school

I hope you've got your thinking cap on

The days of staying up late are gone

It's time to study and take some notes

And memorize some ancient quotes

And make new friends don't be a crab

And sign up for the study lab

It's time to get focused and crack a book

No matter how nerdy it may look.

The Truth

My brother likes to fabricate he's good at telling lies

He'll quickly make up a story before

you can blink your eyes

His head is full of fiction you will never find a fact

Everyone knows he's dishonest and

that's not the way to act

Each time he opens up his mouth

there's a whopper nothing small

He concocts the grandest tales you

see and each one ten feet tall

My brother stays in trouble all the

grownups know his name

He may never see outside again or play a video game

Today he claimed to see a ghost inside a photo booth

My brother likes to fabricate so

you'll never hear the truth.

Today I Got A Valentine

Today I got a Valentine the kind that grownups get

A chocolate covered candy heart I haven't opened yet

A coffee mug, a teddy bear and a shiny bracelet too

A dozen roses in a vase and a card that says I love you

I even got a gift card to my favorite restaurant

Two tickets to a movie now what

else could anyone want

I got so many items I can't fit them on the shelf

My Valentine's Day is always good

when I purchase for myself.

Today I Got Detention

Today I got detention it's not the place to be

All my friends keep pointing, laughing

and making fun of me

My pals will get home sooner but I will be there late

I had plans to catch a movie but I

guess I can cancel that date

Today I god detention you'd think I committed a crime

Now my butt must stay glued to

this seat until its finish time

I cannot eat, can't talk, can't speak

and I cannot pass a note

Next time I'll think before I cheat I do not like this boat

My parents will not be happy, for me this won't go well

For sure I will be grounded, they're

going to take my cell

Today I got detention because I chose to shirk

Next time I think I'll listen and focus on my own work.

What's On The Menu

What's on the menu can you help me please

Do you have lasagna, macaroni and cheese?

Can I tell you my favorite dish?

Cheese on grits with a plate of fish

How about a burger and some fries

Candy, cookies, cakes and pies

Fried chicken, turkey or sausage strings

Do you serve up onion rings?

Shrimps with gravy, beans and ham

Mashed potatoes, candy yam

A slice of meatloaf would be nice

Lemonade with extra ice

Something sour, something sweet

What's on the menu I'm ready to eat.

When The Bell Rings

When the bell rings and the school day is done

We quickly rush home so then we can have fun

We first do our homework then check on our chores

Then eat a lite snack and we're off out the doors

We hang out with friends and we try to have fun

This is our routine when the school day is done.

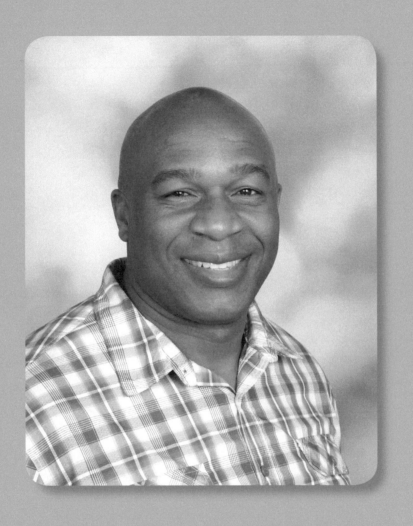

James Langston Jr is a Tampa, FL native and author of Maximus The Musical Elephant. James currently resides in Alpharetta, GA with his family, where he is currently working on more material to spread the joy of reading.